The Insider's Guide To JoyTunes' Piano Maestro

by Becki Laurent

The Insider's Guide to JoyTunes' Piano Maestro

Hi y'all!

If you are reading this book then you have taken the GIANT leap into the world of technology. Or you know me from Facebook and you just want to see what craziness I've wrought NOW! For that I thank you! I know most authors do that whole dedication page, but I'm not really an author. I'm a music teacher. An OLD music teacher.

And this is your Insider's Guide to JoyTunes' Piano Maestro.

Let me begin by saying this is a "choose your own adventure" book. When you get to the end of a chapter or section you may want to skip on over to the section you need. Or you can read beginning to end, inserting your own repeat signs where you like. (One of my favorite composers, Elissa Milne does that. It's her idea. If you don't know her work, STOP and go get it!)

You're back? Here we go!

SOMETHING REALLY IMPORTANT
*Important iPad Basic Function: If you double tap the iPad home button (the circle button located at the bottom of the ipad screen on the actual iPad which I also call the iPad belly button) all your open apps will show as thumbnail pics with their icon below them. You can choose to switch by sliding back and forth between these apps by tapping the pictures.

This means you can read this book. Double tap the belly button and switch to Piano Maestro to see what

I'm talking about. Then double tap and choose iBooks or Kindle app to switch back.

One more thing here and it's really super important. This double tap belly button thing is where you go to CLOSE apps. This is also known as **FORCE CLOSING** an app. From this screen place your finger on the big pic and while you are still making contact with the screen, slide the pic up to the top and off the screen until it disappears with a flicking motion.   You have now done the Microsoft equivalent of "tapping the x in the corner to close". This is the iPad version.

If you already have an iPad:
        Go back to the CONTENTS page and find the section you want.

If you don't have an iPad but are thinking about getting one:
        GO TO SECTION 1.

If you are confused:
        Go get coffee. I will wait here.

Section 1

iPad-what to buy, where to buy, how much to spend, regrets and wishes

iPad. I will forever be grateful to 3 amazing men: my Dad, Hector Tapia, my husband Didier and Steve Jobs. My Dad was the first tech geek I ever knew. Back in the 1970's (before many of you were born and you can't convince me otherwise) my Dad always had computers of some kind around the house. He nurtured my love for music and tech. He gave them to his very young daughter to play with. He encouraged me to be curious and learn how computers worked. He let me take them apart.

My husband Didier gave me a Personal Digital Assistant (PDA) as an engagement gift. My Mom was rather offended that the ring came later but this is a man who knows the way to my heart and I knew I'd found my soul mate. We are raising two adorable techies. We are that couple. The one with His and Her shared online grocery lists. We have His, Her and theirs online calendars. We use the app, Who

Has The Kids, to keep track of our kids. We use Tile to track our children in public places. Yup, that's us.

Steve Jobs created the iPad. I was not a fan of Apple early on. To me it was just another operating system and one that I had not spent any time learning. Sure, the computers were pretty but I never did understand the menus and the trash can icon? That just scared me. The whole ALL IN ONE computer concept was not to be trusted. Those Apple people were odd ducks.   Bill Gates was my guy. TEAM PC! That was me. But I did buy an iPod, which was really handy for carrying around all my music and it was a cool green color.

My husband asked me if I wanted to try the latest Apple gadget. I said: "Sure. What will I use it for?" He said "Well, since it does a lot of the administrative stuff you need for your business you won't be tied to a laptop or desktop." Me: "But it's Apple. They don't write MUSIC EDUCATION APPS. Still, it would be nice to have my calendar, notes and invoices all on a device that fits in my purse." (Little did I know my Windows days were fast coming to a close.) I was SOLD. I'd spent years trying to get my calendar, music class playlists, camera, camcorder and phone numbers into one place so this seemed like the next step. CHANGED. MY. LIFE.   I've retired my Windows computers. I bought a Mac. I'm no longer scared of the trashcan icon. I am TEAM APPLE. If I can do it. You can do it.

Rules for purchasing an iPad

Everyone has his or her own opinions. You are reading my book so HAH! Here are mine.

Rule 1: Pick a size. You should go to a store that sells iPads and pick them up. Literally. Put it in your hands. IPads are sold everywhere. Best Buy, Wal-Mart, Target, Radio Shack... everywhere. There are 3 sizes: Full, Mini and the iPad Pro.

I have an Ipad Air,a mini and the Pro.

I LOVE and ADORE my mini because it's small and slim enough not to force me to change my purse habits. The full size iPad is bigger and requires a new purse or 2 or 4. Whatever. I love it for the days when my allergy eyes are so bad I can't see and I want everything on my screen GIANT. You will often see me with both of them in my hands. Don't judge. The PRO is LIFE CHANGING! I retired my laptop and use the Pro as my laptop now. The speakers are AMAZING. The graphics FANTASTIC and the pencil? WOW! Notating your music in ForScore is a DREAM!

Moving on because I can wax on about how incredible the Pro is for a LONG TIME. It is expensive so I sold a kid and had a bake sale. Just suggestions.

You also have to consider who will be looking at it. If you want students to use it, then probably bigger (read more $) is better. If you aren't sure if you can commit to this relationship, then get the mini. It will still work and it's cheaper. The students will still think you are cool.

Rule 2: Now that you've committed to a size, let us discuss memory. I'm not going to get all-technical here. Basically, Kim Komando says, "buy the most memory you can afford." I will add (since I'm the Piano Digital Goddess) "In the latest model you can afford." The rule in its entirety:

> **Buy the latest model you can afford with the most memory you can afford.**

Here's the thing- most new users are tempted to buy 16 gigs. That's ok. Most teachers I know who have done that have regretted it later. Music Apps are HUGE. You are probably a musician so you listen to a ton of music. You think of these pieces and songs as family members. You'll want to carry them with you. Always. Not just in your heart and mind but ACTUALLY with you. These things use up memory and memory is a precious precious commodity in the iPad world.

As amazing as this device is there is no way to expand the iPad memory on the device. You can't plug in a thumb or flash drive. You can expand it with iCloud (which is basically an external drive you will never see but can connect to and use to store information).

My best advice is to get at least 64 gigs. And here's why. You'll start using it for Piano Maestro. But then you will discover that you can use if for student notes and videos. And then Rhythm apps. And PICTURES. And magazines. And organizing. And Invoices. That's the moment you know that you are addicted. The moment when you think to yourself "I wonder if there's an app for that?" The answer is yes, there is. You will need a ton of memory! Y'all are grownups so buy what you can afford. I am but the voice of options.

Rule 3: Find a Retailer. Please shop around. Open Box deals are available from many places: Amazon & Best Buy are my two first stops. EVERY major retailer has sales so check those out and if you are lucky enough to be purchasing before the NEXT BIG APPLE RELEASE you can get the almost latest model really discounted. You can also go to Apple's website and search for refurbished. Know that Apple refurbishes these, will have a warranty and be just like new. I've purchased several of these and never had a problem. Since these iPads that have been sent back you may have to compromise a bit on style, color, memory or size since they may not have exactly what you want. But you are getting it for a discounted price so there's that.

Rule 4: Piano Maestro does not work on the first generation iPad. Don't get one of those even if it is $50. You won't be able to do anything to it. It will never be any faster because Apple no longer supports the software used to make it work.

GO PURCHASE IT.

When you take it out of the box there will be no instruction manual. No guide of any sort. It's ok. Start pushing buttons and it will turn on and tell you what to do. This is actually a really important discovery. IPads are designed to be "intuitive." That is, you will instinctively know how to make it work. You can't break it by touching the screen or pushing buttons. Don't be scared. Push buttons, flip switches, be fearless.

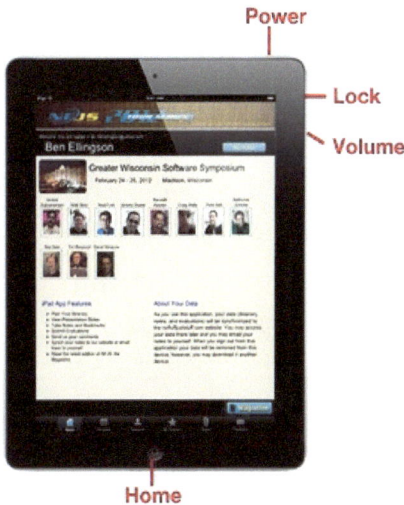

Power

Lock

Volume

Ben Ellingson

Greater Wisconsin Software Symposium

Home

Important note: Be sure that the side oblong switch located on the ipad upper right side corner (lock button) is not showing red. That is your mute button and if it is showing red you most likely won't be able to hear Piano Maestro.

You will be asked to create an iTunes account. You'll need your email and a valid credit card. Be sure you have these things handy. Write down your iTunes user id (also known as your Apple ID) and password.

Put it somewhere safe. Do not share it with anyone. Your iTunes account is the hub of all your activities. It is the location from which you will purchase everything.

Section 2
The iTunes Store

You'll need to download Piano Maestro. To do that you'll need to set up an iTunes account.

Here's the thing: Apple is going to REQUIRE a valid credit card to set up this account. Not JoyTunes, the creators of Piano Maestro.

 If you are reading this then it's very likely that it's because you heard Piano Maestro was free for teachers and their students. It is. Once you set up your Piano Maestro account it will be free but Apple and JoyTunes are 2 different companies.   Apple requires the credit card for apps you purchase. JoyTunes does not. You may NEVER purchase an app from Apple but they take no chances. Once you set up your iTunes account, tap on the App Store icon and find the rectangle with the tiny magnifying glass in it in the upper right corner of iTunes page and type in JoyTunes. All the apps that JoyTunes offers will show on the screen.

Tap on the "GET" under Piano Maestro and it will download to your iPad. When it is done, that box will say "OPEN". Tap it. You won't have to do this every time you want to open the app. It will have it's own icon on your iPad menu screen. It's just easier to do it from here for now.

This is your Piano Maestro opening screen. I had to actually find this image because I haven't seen it in a long time. You won't either unless you log out or have to log in.

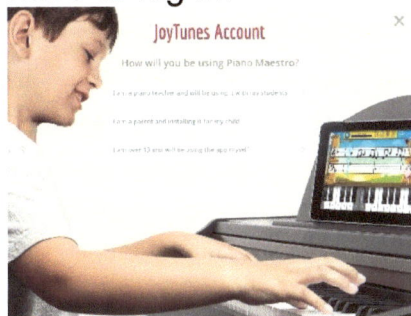

This is a nexus. Your choice will take you to different places. Not in the app itself but in the corridors of JoyTunes and Apple. If you are a teacher and tap that box you will be telling Apple that you do not need to subscribe. Yay! Piano Maestro is free for teachers and their students. Once you go through the "create a log in" process you are officially removed from Apple's view. You will need to create your log in using the email you use most often with your students. This is critical. Whatever email you use will be tagged by JoyTunes at JoyTunes as a teacher. Any students who claim to be students of yours will need your email as "proof".

Read on my friends …. We have begun!

Here are some important notes about the iTunes stores.

That's right, storeS.

There are several of them: the App store for Mac, the app store for iPad, the app store for iPhone. When you download an app from any Apple device, the device will, by default, take you to the store that it is in. If you are on your iPhone and tap the app store icon you will automatically ONLY see the apps available for iPhone. Same thing for the iPads (both the full sizes and the mini's use the same store). The Mac has it's own store too.

Some apps work only on the iPad. Piano Maestro is one of those. Some apps will work on both. Angry Birds is one of those. Some apps, like my favorite for student records, InFocus Pro, only shows in the iTunes iPhone app store, but once you own it you can use it on your iPad too.

Basically it works like this:
IPhone apps: apps work on iPhone but some will work on iPads. The only way to know is to try it out.
IPad apps: work on iPad but might work on iPhone. IPhone apps work on iPad.
Mac apps: only work on a Mac desktop.

For our purposes:

Piano Maestro is iPad and iPad mini only.
Piano Dust Buster 2 is iPad, iPad mini or iPhone.
Simply Piano is, for now, iPhone only but will work on iPad
and iPad mini. *Update: will be in the iPad app store February
2016.
JoyTunes Metronome: iPhone, iPad, iPad mini, Apple watch.

Section 3 Setting up your Piano Maestro Account/Login

The first time you open Piano Maestro you will see a
screen that looks like this and this is where you will
create your JOYTUNES Log In. It's pretty easy. But
first some questions.

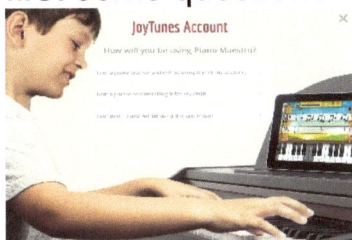

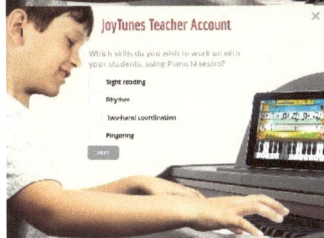

Answer the questions and fill in
the boxes.

Whatever you do- DON'T FORGET WHAT EMAIL and PASSWORD YOU USED. Also, don't use an overly hard for you to remember password. There is no money attached to this particular log in so you don't need to worry that some hacker is going to steal your credit card info.

Please don't use your bank log in password or your email log in password! Those are sacrosanct and should never be used for anything else. *You should make those bank and email passwords long, with capital letters, lower case letters, numbers and symbols.

I don't ever encourage people to use the Facebook log in because I don't actually understand the process and I don't trust Facebook to keep my data secure.

As you go through the set up process Joytunes will ask a few questions that make people nervous. They will ask for your location, phone number and email. I want you to know that JoyTunes will never sell or rent your information (or your student's information) to anyone EVER.

Remember, you are getting Piano Maestro (the single most amazing app created) for FREE. JoyTunes may call upon you to consult or see if you are available to help out at a conference. They may call you to ask you questions about features. They may contact you for a success story. They may just check to make sure you are a teacher. They may contact you because someone contacted them to find a JoyTunes teacher and you happen to be in that same geographical area. What other company leads business to you from an app? I'm sure you understand that they have to protect themselves from people pretending to be teachers to get the awesomeness for free. After all, they have to pay the bills too and I, for one, want them to keep giving me content.

Once you get all logged in, Piano Maestro will ask you to add some students to get started. You can do this one of two ways: 1. You can add a real student, with a real email, age and you can pick an avatar (that's the little picture of the student) and don't forget to pick the lesson date or 2. you can add yourself with no email, pick your avatar and make yourself 20 years younger. Again, don't forget to pick a lesson date. Hit enter.

Some teachers are very worried about privacy issues. I get that. I'm a parent too. JoyTunes does not sell or rent information. Students who have iPads themselves at home can get homework assignments from you (see section 8 Piano Maestro Home Challenges) if you have connected them to your account by email. This is strictly a convenience for you so you don't have to type in the email every time.

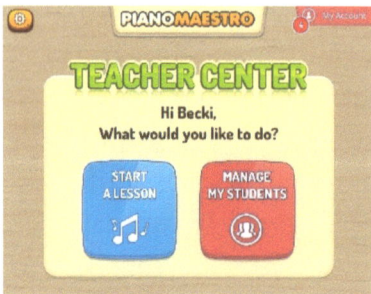

Section 4
Playing Piano Maestro with What?
(AKA What kinds of instruments will Piano Maestro recognize?)

There are basically 2 types of instruments to use. Acoustic (they don't plug in)

Electronic (they do plug in).

Bear with me now.

In the Electronic instrument department we have MORE options. There are Electronic Keyboards and Digital Pianos. The keyboards are usually the smaller 66 key keyboards people give kids for Christmas. The Digital Pianos are full sized keyboards with a thousand different options.

Piano Maestro works with all of these. You get to choose how.

Acoustic Piano
This is the easiest. Take your iPad. Open Piano Maestro and begin to play. Skip to section Playing a song/Piece in Piano Maestro.

Digital Piano
Also pretty easy. See Acoustic Piano Above.

Electronic Keyboard
Again, simple. See Acoustic Piano Above

ADDING MIDI

MIDI stands for Musical Instrument Digital Interface. It's basically standardized sounds for musical instruments. When a computer gets a signal from channel 32, it knows to play the same sound every time. Sort of like standardized nail sizes in carpentry. Which there aren't but wouldn't it be nice if there were?

If you are teacher with a keyboard lab or you have a digital piano and an acoustic piano in your office then this is an option for you. You can have 2 students working at the same time. One works with you on the acoustic piano and one works solo on the digital piano or electronic keyboard. Piano Maestro accepts Midi. If you need to know how to do this skip to section 11 Setting Up with Midi. You'll need some cables.

OTHER INSTRUMENTS

Can Piano Maestro be used with other instruments? Sure!

It's not optimized for those instruments so you may have a little trouble getting things started but once it's started it will evaluate the same way it does for a piano. I've successfully used it with harp, violin, bassoon, guitar, and flute. Really any C instrument is fine. Just don't ask about guitar. I'm the world's meanest guitar teacher ever because my students have to mentally transpose what they see to the corresponding note on the guitar and yes, they have to do that whole octave switch thing.

SPECIAL NOTE ABOUT ACOUSTIC PIANOS

Dearest Teachers. You know that family that found a piano on Craig's List for a steal? The one where the student comes in and says "It doesn't sound like this on my piano." The one you've been begging the family to tune forEVER? THAT ONE?

Take a deep breath. You no longer have to nag. Piano Maestro will not work with an out of tune piano. Let the children do the nagging (because they are expert naggers). They will insist (read, relentlessly nag) that to play Piano Maestro at home the piano must be tuned. To their very own parents. I can't tell you how many times this has happened. And how grateful to JoyTunes I am. Some of these pianos hadn't been tuned in years. And, now, they are!

Incidentally, electronic keyboards and digital pianos sometimes also need to be reset. Button pushers (read the adorable student that comes in and pushes every button on your digital Yamaha) sometimes accidentally transpose the entire keyboard (in micro steps occasionally) and the keyboard or digital piano needs to be reset to factory defaults. Check your owner's manual. Or visit us at our Facebook Page: JoyTunes Teachers and we will get you squared away.

Section 5
PIANO MAESTRO TEACHER'S MAIN MENU

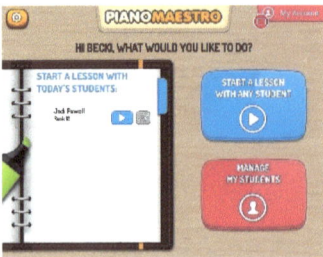

This is what you see when you open Piano Maestro.

You will already have been asked to add a student. Remember that you don't have to add an email to play. You may have already added yourself as a student. Tap a name (yours if you show in the book) or tap "Start a Lesson with Any Student".
In the upper left corner is a little gear. This is setting up options for you. By now you either LOVE the Piano Maestro Theme song or you don't. Personally, I LOVE IT. It's my ring tone too. You can turn it off if you want. This page also has a really important tool for teachers who travel. The 3rd button down says "Manage OFFLINE CONTENT".

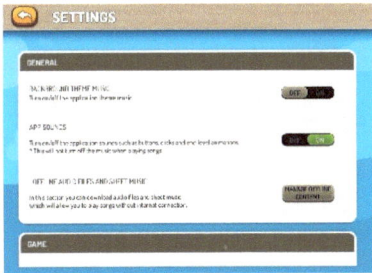

This is a super cool feature the JoyTunes development team added for teachers who need to use Piano Maestro in a place with no Wi-Fi. Usually, when you play Piano Maestro the app downloads the background tracks for songs as you use them.

Once they are on your iPad you will always have them.

However, if you wanted to download a whole section of the library for use for a whole bunch of students or just because WIFI is sketch and unpredictable- just get yourself somewhere with a good signal and download the sections you need. I recommend just doing a few sections at a time because some of these sections are deceptively content rich. Don't close the app because it will stop. Just let it run and go play Candy Crush on your phone.

Start a Lesson with Today's Students

You will see a list of the students you have on that day or the book will be closed. Pick the student you want to work with and tap the blue button to get started.

Now jump to section 8 in this book.

You can always tap "start a class with any student". This is also where you go when you want to manage your students. This option allows you to scroll through your students and pick the one you want. Simply tap that student's name and you're in.

You can also access Add/Manage Students from here too. You don't need to add yourself as a student if you don't want to because you can tap the explore button located next to your name at the top of this screen. I don't do this because I like to play as a student.

True confession: I think I have 3 profiles: a beginner, an intermediate and a Maestro Rank!

ADDING OR DELETING STUDENTS
You may want to add or delete a student. Do that here.

If you tap the Red Manage My Students button you can add or delete students. To add a student: tap the plus sign and follow the instructions. To delete a student just tap the "remove" and all the students will have a "delete" button next to their names. Pick the student you want to delete. Tap the button.

In this section you will see:
a. which students are connected
b. which students are not connected

c. if the student's name is in yellow, you are waiting for a response.

d. A request to connect from a student.

Beware requests to connect! Sometimes people will find your email and try to connect to you so they can get the app for free. Please do not accept requests from people you do not know or are not part of your studio. The free feature is for teachers and their students. ONLY!

In the upper right corner is a red MY ACCOUNT tab. Tapping that button gives you access to all YOUR important profile information.

You can change your email by tapping the pencil next to your current email address. I have really bad eyes. Like stack 3 bottle bottoms together and that's my GOOD eye. I never can see the little gray pencil.

You can connect to Facebook if you like. Don't worry! Your students will not be connected to Facebook. This is only so you can use your Facebook profile picture as your avatar because you don't want to be the little old lady or a kid.

At the bottom of this page is a short cut to your STUDENT PROFILES. Also shown here is the all-important SUPPORT tab and a couple other buttons you can explore on your own. The only other button I want to chat about is the SUPPORT tab.

SUPPORT TAB

You will NEVER EVER EVER find another app company as responsive as JoyTunes. EVER! Honestly, I don't even think they are human. They almost always answer within hours of a question and if you post on their Facebook page it might be seconds for a response. This is also where you will find the FAQ's.

There are two items here which are all kinds of important: the Send Message (in green) and the Reset MusicSense ENGINE (in grey).

The send message is basically your "PLEASE HELP ME!" support ticket. When you tap it an email form will automatically appear. There is a tag which is already embedded. Write out your problem with as many details as possible, screen shots if you can and hit send. Don't delete the tag or they won't know what to fix.

RESET MUSICSENSE ENGINE is super important to use if Piano Maestro suddenly stops hearing your piano. This is what you push so the app can "relearn" to listen to your piano. When you tap it you won't see anything change. NADA! The action is internal and is super fast so tap it a couple times if it makes you feel better. I always do.

Tap the x in the upper right corner to return to your student list.

To continue: SELECT A STUDENT FROM YOUR LIST!

Section 6
PLAYING A Song/Piece in Piano Maestro

This is, in my inflated opinion, the absolute GOLD STANDARD of Music Education Apps. I've been using tech in music lessons since the early 90's. This makes me like 535 years old in tech years. I've had to learn to program. I've had to learn to take my computer apart (my husband was horrified) and install new graphics cards, new sound cards and various other parts. I've had to learn all about Midi cables and various assorted other cables. I've spent LIFETIMES on HOLD with Tech Support! It's been quite an education. I often wonder if maybe I should have double majored in Electrical Engineering! It would certainly have helped. And along came JoyTunes.

With Piano Maestro you don't need cables.

Take a moment. Appreciate that sentence.

When you select a song to play you see this screen:

You tap play and you see a screen like this:

image 1

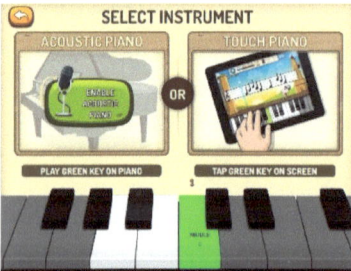

Or this: **image 2**

Ok- In **image 1** you have some choices. Choose your own adventure, right?

If **you want to play the piece on the iPad**, then tap the TOUCH PIANO box on the right. This forces you to use the iPad as your piano. It's a nice feature for the littles or for when you don't have a piano handy. I use it all the time while I'm sitting in the airport, but only if the song/piece has keys the size shown in image 1.

If you want to play the piece/song on your actual real live instrument, then you need to tell the iPad that's what you want to do by tapping the box that says "ENABLE ACOUSTIC PIANO". This is the command to the iPad to turn on the mic and listen. Then you need to play the HIGHLIGHTED KEY (in image 1, that's Middle C) on the REAL piano. It's listening to you now so it's waiting to hear the correct pitch from the instrument.

Image 2 doesn't have the "enable acoustic piano" choice. Why? Because you've already chosen it and Piano Maestro remembered. In this case, the only thing that changes is the button is missing.
In Image 2: if you want to play on the iPad embedded piano, tap the box that says TOUCH PIANO. I wouldn't do this for this piece. Those keys are tiny and my fingers don't fit. In some pieces that button is locked so you can't do it even if you want to. I really love that they did that!

In **Image 2**: if you want to play on your piano then all you have to do is play the highlighted key on your piano and you are good to go!

Go to Journey and select Chapter 1 Rocking.
Choose your instrument: piano or iPad. Tap Play.

Tap the starting key either on the piano or on the iPad.

Once the music starts you will see the music begin to scroll across the screen. Listen to the backing track and play along with that. When the note gets to the beat closest to the blue line play it on the piano. And keep going.

Try not to watch the metronome. This is hard for those of us trained to always watch the metronome peripherally. There is actually a micro second lag in playing with Piano Maestro that is just noticeable to experienced pianists but kids don't notice it at all. Remember that the iPad has to hear what you are playing and process it. That takes a smidge of time. You'll get used to it.

Once you complete the song you will get points and stars. You can continue if you are happy with your score or play it again if you needed some work on your timing or notes. Hopefully you didn't have any trouble with Rocking since it's only middle C.

Section 7
Getting Connected
Visualize yourself as a Wrangler. The cowboy kind. While the world revolves around you, you throw out a lasso and snag someone. And then you throw out

more lassoes. This is what we are attempting to do here.

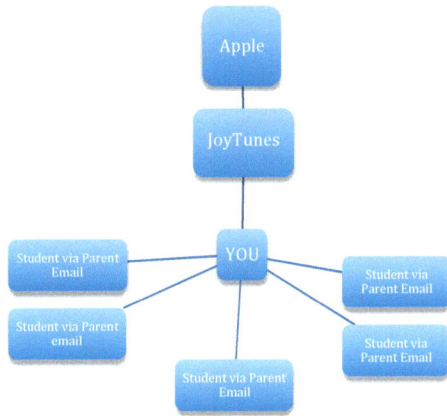

Apple connects you to JoyTunes when you download Piano Maestro. You (TEACHER) connect to JoyTunes when you use Piano Maestro. When you add students, they are in your account.

When you add a student's parent's email you are essentially FLAGGING that email address for JoyTunes. That is, you are HIGHLIGHTING JoyTunes servers to recognize that email as JOYTUNES FAMILY when a log in request is created. I can't stress enough how important it is to realize what's happening here because this is where most mistakes in connecting happen. It's all about the emails.

I have an email address for me. I've had it for years. I have email addresses that I only use for my business. I even own an encrypted email address that can't be hacked, tracked or commercialized. I own domain names too for my kids, my businesses and my family name. I have email addresses for those. I have at least a dozen email addresses. My studio parents only know one of these.   I send all my parents invitations to download Piano Maestro from my studio email address.   I sent those invitations to the same email address I use for their invoices. And here's what happens.

Mom of my student, sitting at the computer, reading her email: "Honey, we got an invitation from the piano teacher to download an app? Can you do that please? Its called Piano Maestro. Search JoyTunes in the app store and it will come up."   Dad of my student, sitting in the living room, using the ipad: "OK."

Dad finds the app in the App store and proceeds to download. Dad opens the app. Dad to Mom: "I got it. Now what?" Mom: "Sign us up."

MAYDAY! STOP! RIGHT HERE IS THE MISCOMMUNICATION! THIS MOMENT RIGHT HERE!

Dad opens app and creates a log in using HIS EMAIL. Which is not one I EVEN KNOW because I've never sent him anything and I've only ever even seen him at recitals for like, 3 seconds.

HERE IS A PROBLEM. JoyTunes believes they have a new customer. A CUSTOMER who they view as a subscriber (read, must pay for the subscription to Piano Maestro @ $9.99 per month, Apple sees this too and rejoices!) because his email is not flagged as JOYTUNES FAMILY or technically, CONNECTED TO A TEACHER. HER email is flagged as CONNECTED TO A TEACHER.

The next month, Dad notices that the family credit card through Apple's iTunes store is being charged $9.99 per month for Piano Maestro.

I get an email from Dad (this is the first time he's ever emailed me and I promptly put his contact information into my contacts).
"Dear Ms. Becki, HI! Hope this email finds you well. WHY AM I BEING CHARGED FOR AN APP $120 per YEAR when you told my wife it would be FREE?"

And so, I begin the process of unraveling this situation. I find out that they created their log in with a different email. NOW, we have to connect manually from the account they have already created so JoyTunes knows that this NEW, I'VE NEVER SEEN IT BEFORE EMAIL is actually JoyTunes Family.

CONNECTING TO A TEACHER FOR AN ACCOUNT SET UP BY A PARENT

Well, now that we know what happened. Let's fix it.
I have the parent bring the iPad in.

Steps 1-6 below happen on the student's iPad.

Step 1: I open the My Account Tab in the Upper Right Corner.
Step 2: Tap on the child's name under profiles. A screen will appear on the right that has a green button that says "Connect to Teacher". When you tap it a search box will appear.

Step 3: Type in your email in the search box. You should use the same email you used to create your log in for Piano Maestro.

Step 4: You will be asked "Connect to teacher?" Say yes!

Step 5: This iPad needs to wait for a response from you (Teacher) from your account on your iPad.

Step 6: The parents need to go to their iTunes account and cancel the subscription to Piano Maestro. Here's the link: https://support.apple.com/en-us/HT202039 or they can Google "Manage my iTunes subscriptions". They need to follow Apple's instructions to turn off auto renew. They also need to be told that Apple will send them 1 gazillion emails telling them that "THEIR SUBSCRIPTION WILL NOT RENEW!" in a panicky Apple tone. They also need to be told to ignore those emails. They won't be charged again and Apple will be a sad apple. It's ok. They will get over it.

What You Need to do Next:
Steps 1-4 below happen on YOUR ipad.

Step 1: Open Piano Maestro on your iPad.

Step 2: In the My Account Tap, you will see a blinking red button.

Step 3: Open My ACCOUNT by tapping on it.

Step 4: You will see a "Request to Connect" Tap Accept.

You have now told JoyTunes that this is an approved (manually by you) email and they can have the content for free.

Does this seem like a lot of trouble? It is.

I always tell my parents "When you create that log in, use the Email address I use to communicate with you or you WILL BE CHARGED because JoyTunes will NOT KNOW WHO YOU ARE." I stress the importance of this A LOT. In my TEACHER VOICE. Not the "you're in trouble" voice but the "YOU ARE NOT GOING TO MAKE THIS HARD ON ME, PAY ATTENTION!" voice.

Now we have this:

```
v------------------------------------v
JoyTunes----Teacher—Parent
```

And the circle is complete.

Now, there is one last step. Both sides need to force close the app and reopen Piano Maestro. (See chapter Getting Started) Again, remember that the only way JoyTunes servers know what is going on is if you close Piano Maestro completely and reopen it. Not delete and reinstall. Just do a normal force close "close because I'm done using it". This action stores all the current progress in the cloud and when someone opens the account, Piano Maestro gets that information pushed to whoever opens it next.

One more insider tip

Sometimes people will find out that Piano Maestro is free for registered teachers and their students. They will search for a teacher using an address found from your studio info online. These people, who are not your students, will send you a request to connect. The hope is that you will accept, no questions asked. I beg you not to do this. It is a very great privilege that JoyTunes has given us. We must take care not to abuse it. Please do not accept a request to connect from a student you don't personally know. Thank you.

Section 8
Piano Maestro Home Page Details

This is where you start with your students. This is their account. We also call this a student's profile. Each student has their own profile and all their progress is tracked individually. You will see 3 pictures: Journey, Library and Home Challenges.

It's easiest to start with Journey to learn to play a song. Once you get the steps down you can apply them to every song in the app.

If you want you can skip to Section 6 Playing A Song/Piece in Piano Maestro.

Continue reading this chapter if you want more details.

Teachers always ask if they can make themselves a student so they can see what the students sees. This is what the student sees. The only difference between your account and theirs is the number of profiles in the account tab. Otherwise it is EXACTLY the same.

THE JOURNEY

The Journey is a piano teaching curriculum. It is divided into chapters and each chapter is locked until you play and master the concepts it contains. No you cannot cheat. No there are no cheat codes. (I know because I scoured the Internets looking for them.) You must play and master the skills required to continue. There are, at the time of this writing, 37 chapters. Each chapter builds a little more skill.

Teachers can see the concepts covered in each chapter under the title of the chapter. The arrows on the left and right of the screen move you back and forth between chapters.

In the upper right corner is a "FAST FORWARD" test. This is like a short cut to allow students who are not beginners to get to more appropriate levels. You can take these sight-reading tests to unlock chapters and move forward. These are PASS or FAIL. Do or DO NOT. There is no try. You must earn 90% or better in notation and timing to pass. You can't practice them either because I looked all over for sheet music of these tests or it doesn't exist.

THE LIBRARY
The Library has 3 sections: SONGS, EXERCISES and METHODS. I cannot even tell you how much I love this part of the app because just when you think it can't get better? The Dev team makes it better!

Songs
When you tap Songs it takes your right to categories. You choose. There are over 5000 songs and works in this library so you have oodles of choices. The current list is:

Recently Played- a list of songs you just played

Free- a list of songs available to people who have downloaded but have not subscribed

Christian Contemporary- songs that are all the current favorites of praise and worship bands

Classical & Opera- songs and pieces that are standard for competitions, however, they may not be the full versions

Holiday- includes all types of holiday tunes, sacred and secular

Kids & Folk- some nice songs to sing along with

Musicals- MY FAVORITE SECTION! Songs and tunes from popular musicals like The Sound Of Music and Grease.

Pop & Rock- the student's favorite section, which includes songs from artists, like Taylor Swift, Bruno Mars, Maroon 5, Justin Bieber. Thankfully, they find these all by themselves and I don't have to listen to Bieber music in class! Bullet dodged!

Summer Camp- Summer camp only shows up during the summer. See section Summer Camp below.

TV & Game Themes- Game of Thrones, Happy from Despicable Me and Angry Birds plus many more. This is the student's 2nd Favorite place to play!

The songs at the top of the list are always the easiest versions. Swiping up takes you to the bottom of the list where there are harder versions of the songs. The Content Director and his team often do 3 or 4 versions of each song so students of all levels can play. You can find these by tapping on the Levels tab and choosing a level. I don't do that too often because it really limits what you see. An example would be Happy (from Despicable Me). It is available in Easy, Melody line only (especially useful for C instrument players) and an intermediate version. This is a teacher-influenced area. Teachers asked that songs be added with multiple versions so everyone at any level would be able to play. The Dev team listened and agreed. :)

(Yes. I know. Not supposed to use emoticons in a legit book. Mr. Kolinek did explain the rules. Y'all are lucky I waited this long to do it. I smile a lot.)

You can search for particular songs by using the search bar with the magnifying glass in the upper right corner.

Exercises
Tap the Exercise button and all your Happy Piano Teacher cells will sing! Scale exercises, rhythm, intervals, coordination ….. Ahhh! All right there at your finger tips! Assign away my friends! Here too, you can select exercises by key or by hands. Simply tap the tabs at the top.

You'll notice that some of the exercises are only in the key of C. This is because they were added early in Piano Maestro development and the team was unsure whether teachers would like them or not. HAHAHAHAHA! As if we don't love exercises? Once the teachers saw how valuable these were, they pleaded for MORE. Which, we got.

In most cases you can select your exercise, then select your key. Not all keys are yet represented because it's still a work in progress.

If you notice something is missing, be sure and ask for it on the JTT page.

Methods
Tap the Methods box and your digital library appears. Piano Maestro features popular method books. Alfred's Premier Piano Course, Alfred's Basic Piano Library, Music for Little Mozart's, Irina Gorin's Tales of a Musical Journey and Jennifer Eklunds' Piano

Pronto. Supplemental music for all levels by Tom Gerou, Daniel McFarlane, Bradley Sowash and some of our Amazing teachers! Here are the links if you want to order the hard copies of the books since you obviously can't write on your iPad screen and your student may need an actual book. OK. SHOULD HAVE AN ACTUAL BOOK!

www.alfred.com
www.pianopronto.com
www.gorinpianotales.org
www.supersonicspiano.com

*Update These links are now included in Piano Maestro when you open the book and play the songs! YAY!

Feel free to check out the music in Piano Maestro. All the tracks are legit and every song in the book is in the app completely and wholly. There are no in app purchases. This is all yours to examine and play and assign and love.

I love this section because when I need to move a student laterally because they just need a little "seasoning" this is my first stop.

For those of you wondering about the Faber Piano Adventure books? They are not in Piano Maestro. JoyTunes asked me to select pieces of the enormous library and break it down for you by Piano Adventures Units so you can assign songs that correlate with the concepts taught in the Piano Adventures units. These are not the songs in the books but rather songs that complement those taught in those units. Yup! I made most of that (Yigal edited) and I'm currently working to update this to include the recently added scales and exercises! Stay tuned!

The actual method books in the library are Piano Pronto, Alfred's Premier Piano Course, Alfred's Basic Piano Course, Music for Little Mozarts and Irina Gorin's Tales of A Musical Fairy Tale.

If you use these methods then you know that not all the books are included in the library. Why, you ask? There are 2 reasons.

Reason 1 is actually an Apple thing. While the iPad is really powerful it still can't process more than 4 notes at a time. JoyTunes dev team can. iPad can't listen and process more than 4 yet. Maybe the iPad Pro will be able to but JoyTunes hasn't shared that with me. My fingers are crossed. Toes too. *Update As of this edit, the Dev Team is just about ready to crack the polyphony problem that will allow us more than 4 notes and a time and allow the iPad to hear the entire range of the piano. Testing is ongoing but we are closer than ever!

Reason 2 is the amazing Dev team just hasn't had time to add more books. They are the hardest working people I've ever met. Still, it takes an enormous effort to get a book into Piano Maestro. It's not just load a file and add the backing track. Each piece or song has to be broken down into learn modes, checked for tempos, entered in multi keys if necessary. That stuff takes time.

Another thing I noticed from teacher questions on the Facebook page (you did remember to join right?) are requests for specific methods. Music Tree for example. Well, here are some criteria to remember. The method book needs to have its own backing tracks. If you love a particular method and the composer hasn't already created backing tracks it's very unlikely that we can have it in Piano Maestro. JoyTunes doesn't create method book backing tracks. They only do their own content. The composers themselves have to hire out to get those backing tracks.

At the bottom of this page is a section "OR PLAY A SONG RECOMMENDED ESPECIALLY FOR YOU!" These songs are automatically chosen for players based on their location in the journey. If you have a student who is intermediate and hasn't played in the journey much because they could not contain themselves and jumped right into the library because UPTOWN FUNK is their most favorite song, then these songs will be hilariously easy for them. They have to move up through the Journey chapters to have this section match their abilities.

HOME CHALLENGES
The House icon is STUPENDOUS! Granted, this button only works if your student has a Piano Maestro account on his/her iPad at home (and is connected to you) but if they do...WOWZERS! You

can pick any song from the app and tap the house icon and ZAP! It will show up on THEIR ipad without you having to do a single thing more.

Here's a link to view:
https://youtu.be/T0_zWD4YtTQ

See? It's super fast. Like, push a button, fast.

Some things you should note here. First, you will need to force close your iPad at the end of the day to sync your account with the JoyTunes servers. Your student should do this at home when they are finished playing as well. You may need to teach them how. Every time you force close and reopen you sync Piano Maestro. This is the easiest way to get updates too.

If you forgot how to force close, see section GETTING STARTED.

SUMMER CAMP

Ah! The long lazy days of summer. JoyTunes understands that lots of students take the summer off. We, teachers, know that this is not a good thing. Skills need to be sharpened. Brains need stimulation to grow. Chlorine and coconut are awesome summer smells and remind us of what great times we have next to the pool but that doesn't help our piano students remember everything we taught them FOR A WHOLE YEAR. Enter JoyTunes' Summer Camp.

Summer Camp is a contest. For 6-8 weeks during the summer, JoyTunes will release a new song once per week. It's usually one of the big summer hit songs but sometimes it's an oldie but goodie. Students can play these songs for a chance to win gift cards. Yup! JoyTunes gives away legit prize money to 2 lucky winners every week.

To qualify for a chance to win, you must play the song and get 3 stars. You get entered into the random drawing every time you play and get 3 stars. Someone on the JoyTunes team puts all the contestants into an app that randomly selects 2 winners. Those 2 winners are notified by email and announced via Twitter and Facebook.

When Summer Camp is over all the songs are relocated to their respective categories. You can access them and continue to play.

Section 9
PRACTICE OPTIONS!
This is another one of those features that just makes this app AMAZING!

To get to the screen below start to play a song and tap the PAUSE button in the upper left corner. (Is it just me or does it seem like there's a lot of stuff in this app?) When you pause the piece (either by tapping the music as it scrolls or using the 2 vertical lines universal pause icon) this menu appears.

CHANGING TEMPOS

Placing your finger and sliding the button left or right under the Metronome Icon will slow it down in percentages. NOT MM MARKINGS! You can't control it very precisely either. It's a percentage of the performance tempo. I'm not good at math but say the piece is mm 100. (See that? I'm using a base 10 number because I'm REALLY TERRIBLE AT MATH.) When you slide that button to the left and it says -12%. That's 12% slower than MM 100 or MM 88. But it won't say MM 88. It will just say -12%. Yup! I can see eyes glazing from here. Sorry about that.

CHOOSE HAND

You can also encourage your students to learn a piece hands separately. How many times have we said that in class? Simply slide the button left or right to select a hand. How many times have we seen the eye roll? If Steve Jobs asks them to do it- NADA! They do it happily.

HOLD ON

Hold on is a great great feature for those students who are just learning a piece and need a moment to think. When you trigger this feature the music will stop and wait for the correct note, and then it will highlight the correct note until it is played. Some students love this, some not so much. I like having options.

NOTE NAMES

On this page you have a short cut to adding note names to the notes as the music scrolls across. Insider note: it took 3 weeks to decide on a suitable font, countless hours of discussions and phone calls to teachers requesting preferences. It's the little things, right?

You can do this in your main settings (that's the little gear under the Note Names toggle switch). Did I mention I was the meanest teacher in the world? My students are not even allowed to look in this direction.

I tell them that I've had JoyTunes turn that feature off completely for my account. The little ones believe me. The big ones are too scared to check.

Last thing to know, anytime you use any of these practice options your maximum allowed Star Collection drops. The exception being tempo changes from 7%-12%. There's no penalty if you slow it down in that range. Everything else is going to cost you stars. For example, playing just your left hand often drops your maximum attainable score to 1.5 stars. Using Hold On takes off MORE! Be sure and let your students know of this because they may have a super perfect play through using hold on, note names and -20% but they will not get 3 stars. They will only get 1 star, maybe less. They will see a screen that says FINAL SCORE CARD. You'll notice the 3 boxes on the left are NOTES, TIMING and ASSISTS. If you use the assists at all that percentage will lower your overall score. Assists are all of the Practice Options.

   If they get 3 STARS- they can SHARE THE MOMENT! See Section 14 SHARE THE MOMENT to find out what that is!

LEARN MODE

The LEARN button is super cool. You know how you send your student home and you HOPE and PRAY that they will remember what you taught them? The process of breaking down the song into sections and by hands is critical to learning a piece, right? The LEARN button does that for you. They have to learn the sections to unlock the next section. Once they've master the song in steps they can play it at full tempo. Thank you JoyTunes Development team! Henceforth I will call them the DEV DUDES!

You can unlock all the learn levels by playing through the song once. Then you can select the portion of the song that is giving them the most trouble. It's not always necessary to use learn mode in its entirety.

Section 10

Transposing in Piano Maestro

Seriously. I was really mad when I discovered this. Not the transposing feature. Because that is awesome and amazing and NO OTHER app does it like this. No. I was mad that they DIDN'T ANNOUNCE IT! I had to find it all by myself. Ugh!

You may or may not (I didn't) have noticed that the title boxes have fractions next to the stars. 3/9, 2/12, like that? This means that the song is available in several different keys. In the brown Song title box in the bottom right corner it says "KEY OF C" or it has a number. If it has a number then that song is available in other keys. Angry Birds, for example, is available in 3 keys. To access the other keys: look in the title box for the long beige rectangle that says "Key of G#m or whatever" and tap it. A drop down menu will show you the additional keys you can select to play.   Tap and scroll up and down to select any one of them and play in that key. This is great for students who are learning a new key and need lots of additional content to reinforce the brain expansion.

Keep in mind that Piano Maestro does not auto tune to your piano. It is A-440. If your piano is out of tune Piano Maestro won't work. Wait. Why is she putting this here? Because I often get told "Please ask the Dev Dudes to make Piano Maestro adjust to my piano!" Even if it could be done (and if anyone could it'd be them) they'd also have to adjust every single backing track too. Some of these backing tracks contain vocals. It would just be too hard to auto detect the tuning of every piano out there and have it match the studio session recordings of these backing tracks. Did I mention that they don't use samples or synths? They use actual people and real instruments to play! Alon (one of the instrumentalists/song arranger/genius) plays gazillions of instruments! And he sings. Everyone on the dev team sings and/or plays. 'Cause they're awesomesauce like that!

Section 11
Setting Up with Midi

Teachers are amazing people. In an effort to expand time we come up with all sorts of creative ideas for making lessons more efficient. Tech time, lab time, extended classes are all things we do to add value to our lessons.

Back in the day, we used desktop computers and programs like Music Ace, (coming soon to iPad! YAY! Like, 2016! SUPER GIANT YAY!), MidiSaurus and if you are REALLY OLD (like me!) The Miracle Piano Teaching system. These were wonderful programs. Teachers set them up at a desk in their offices and students were able to learn theory and sight-reading with headphones. Many of these programs require teacher supervision, which is kind of a problem. Piano Maestro does not usually. Once you teach the student to manage their own education, they can learn on their own. If they don't have an iPad then the best thing to do is to have them hang out in your office for 15 minutes post lesson and work on Piano Maestro. Make sure you charge a tech fee for using your ipad. (Google Jennifer Foxx and read her blogs!) Since you will probably need to connect your digital piano or keyboard to your iPad.

BIG UPDATE
All of this has changed with the iOS9 update. You can no longer use the Apple USB connector kit with any amount of reliability. It may or may not work. The issue is Apple limited the amount of power that can be drawn from the iPad for accessory devices. You must now purchase which ever of these cables match your device!

Good news and bad news! Good news is that you only need one cable now! The bad news is might be a bit hard to find!

I bought the old style rig for my little keyboard. I got it at Guitar Center. Whatever you do DO NOT go into Guitar Center and say: "I need to connect my iPad to a keyboard. They will more than likely look at you like you are from Mars and say, "it can't be done!"

Then you have to give them a pitying look and say "Yes, dear heart. It can. Ms. Becki says so." I have an older model Clavinova and it has the MIDI IN/MIDI OUT round pins. If you have one like this you have to remember the MIDI IN on the CABLE gets attached to the MIDI OUT on the keyboard. The MIDI OUT on the CABLE gets attached to the MIDI IN on the keyboard. Opposites attract. True for people and Midi Connections. The iConnectMidi1 is the only cable we have tested that works EVERYTIME! Just be sure to get the cable that matches your iPad.

Amazon Iconnectivity Link:

iConnectMIDI1
by iConnectivity
Link: http://amzn.com/B00MRFG3WU

iConnectMIDI1
by iConnectivity
Link: http://amzn.com/B00D77A8VO

For newer model digital pianos and keyboards you only need a USB printer cable. Shoot me now. USB printer cables only cost like $3. The midi in/out cable

$40 to $60. So, no, we can't be friends if you only need a USB cable. This set up may or may not work because you have to use the Apple USB connector kit. Crap shoot one way or the other. Good luck! I bought new cables. Ouch! But it works.

(This is how I manage my friend list. Just so you know. I base our relationship on your cables.)

My friend David Love did a YouTube video. Here's a link: https://youtu.be/y5aqSTePBw

When we set up for a booth show we always have a small keyboard with a Midi Controller so you can see how they connect. Please visit us at MTNA!   We have two headphones attached to the iPad. We used a simple headphone splitter (Radio Shack $4.99) so 2 people can listen at once. You can also do that in your lab.

For the record I am a Yamaha girl. I have Clavinovas and I love them. I bought the iRig because I needed a small travel keyboard. It's great and has traveled all over with me. As soon as I can though I'm going to get either a Korg Midi Controller or an XKey because they are both slimmer and cooler looking.   And they fit better in my purse. Purses are my life.

Section 12
Social Media and JoyTunes

You say social media and all kinds of boogeymen come into your brain to play. You either love it or hate it. You either find it helpful, distracting, tedious or all of the above. I'm going to discuss the traditional meaning of social media and the Piano Maestro meaning of social media.

Traditional Social Media

This is Facebook, Twitter, Instagram and Snapchat. JoyTunes has a public Facebook page for anyone to go to see announcements and updates. They also have a JoyTunes Teacher page (JTT). If you have a Twitter account you can follow them at JoyTunesCom. Please add yourself to all these communication links. It's the quickest easiest way to get notified of new song or method releases. Plus, they have an awesome sense of humor so you'll see music jokes too!

Social Media by JoyTunes and Piano Maestro

This is a whole different apple. Or maybe it's a watermelon. Social means to connect with people. JoyTunes believes (I'm so glad too!) that parents should be part of the learning experience. Take that in for a moment. How many times do we find parents just dropping kids and going to the grocery store? Or they are deployed overseas? Or the just miss that one moment? The JoyTunes solution is Share the Moment. You can see more details on this in Section 14.

When a student earns 3 stars on a song a Post Card will pop up. This only happens for the first song played in each session. You can hit the Share the Moment button on from the score screen too but only if its 3 stars. Kids can pose and you take a picture with your iPad. This creates a Share the Moment postcard. It is a picture and an mp3 file. You can send it to parents. When they open their email they can see the postcard and listen to the performance. These are all saved on a page in the JoyTunes servers. Anytime they go to listen all the songs ever sent will show. Some parents send these to grand parents, overseas friends and families. I know a couple teachers sent them to themselves and created cd's out of the mp3 and gave them away as Christmas presents. I had each child play 1 or 2 Christmas songs and sent them to the parents the week before Christmas Break with a sweet Holiday Message. For subsequent 3 Star Performances you will have to trigger the STM postcard by tapping the button in the lower left side of the screen.

Insider notes about this: 1. THIS INFORMATION IS NEVER SOLD OR RENTED. You never have to worry that your student's information is going to be given away. **2.** This is not a video. It's only audio. 3. YOU MUST BE CAREFUL TO BE QUIET WHEN THEY ARE PLAYING! Otherwise your dulcet tones will be heard in the background while you shout "COME IN!" and your student is concentrating very hard on a clean performance. Then you get an email from the parent saying "That was lovely. Really, he did a great job! Do you think maybe he could play it again but without you shouting in the background?" That was a hypothetical, of course. I'm just telling you it COULD happen.

The other way JoyTunes uses social media is on their JoyTunes teacher Facebook page. I have to tell you that I've been teaching for like 500 computer years. (Those are like dog years but they accumulate faster.) I had no idea there were groups devoted to piano teachers, piano teachers who teach with Android, piano teachers who teach with iPads, piano teachers who teach with Technology, piano teachers who refuse to teach with anything but books. There are Facebook groups for every conceivable group you can possibly imagine. JoyTunes' Teacher group is AMAZING!

The JoyTunes Teacher group has teachers who have been using Piano Maestro since it was Piano Mania (me) all the way to piano teachers who just purchased their iPad 20 minutes ago and are getting started. This group will answer your questions in seconds, usually. The teachers are knowledgeable but more important the JoyTunes Development team haunts this page. If you find a bug or a glitch, post it here. They will see it and respond. If you have a suggestion for a new song? Post it here. They will add it to their To Do list. (Which, incidentally I'd always imagined to be a giant white board but it's not. It's digital. Of course it is. They are an app company! They use the web based service ASANA. If you are a studio with a staff- you should be using it too.) The list is long but they keep knocking it down! YAY!

Included in every Facebook page is a section called FILES. It's located under the name of the page. JoyTunes uses this section to give teachers all kinds of valuable-you won't find it anywhere else- artwork, charts, lists and helpful tips. Not only that but teachers like the incomparable Lorie Burningham add their artwork and charts and posters for competitions that they created and use with her students. She created a Piano Maestro World Series which is spectacular. All of that is available for you to use. No strings attached.

See? Social Media is not a bad thing. Get involved!

Section 13
PRINTING IN PIANO MAESTRO
This is all legal-schmegal stuff. There's good news and bad news.

The good news: YES YOU CAN PRINT PIANO MAESTRO MUSIC. You can actually do this from 2 places. You can go to www.joytunes.com and look in the resources section and click the curriculum link. That will show you a list of all the original content that is available for print. You can click the link and print the piece. You can also when you open those files, save them to your drop box so you don't have to hunt for them later. I spent like 30 minutes doing that. But now I don't need those files because...

MORE GOOD NEWS! You can print from the app itself. If you tap on the sheet music snippet in the title box you will find the print symbol in the upper right corner. Tap and go. You can choose to print or you can choose to email. This is especially handy for kids who don't have iPads and need to work on something during the week so they can bust out the 3 stars when they come back for their next lesson.

Some caveats though. You will need to have an air printer. That's the printer that prints from your device to your wireless printer. You can also email it to yourself or a parent and they can print from whatever printer they have set up.

The BAD NEWS.

No you cannot print copyrighted music. So, sadly, no Taylor Swift or Bruno Mars. Nor can you print anything from the method books but that's okay because you can BUY those from the composer's websites. See section 8 The Library, Methods for the links to the websites.

<<Pick your song. See the music snippet? Tap it to see the sheet music.

Tap the sheet music!>>

See the Green Rectangle with the out arrow under the Orange X? That's your printer button. Tap it to see the screen below! Then decide what you want to do.

Section 14
Nifty Other Piano Maestro Morsels

This section is going to be all about the extra stuff that JoyTunes gives teachers. One of the best things about this company is that they really listen to what teachers say and implement as many of the ideas we request as they can.

Share the Moment

   The first time they told me about Share the Moment I thought it was inspired genius! There is that moment that every teacher has when you watch the face of a student who has successfully mastered a skill they thought they would never be able to master and they finally get it. That look! It's a privilege I never take for granted. Parents are in a hurry. They are busy with jobs and providing for the family and stress. They don't ever get to really SEE what you and I see as we go about our job of opening the mind and finding the greatness. They don't get to see the beauty of musical success. Share the Moment lets them in on that very cool moment.

   Let's say your student has just successfully played "Chandelier" (That's quite an accomplishment because I can never get 3 full stars on that one!) They finally breathe again because they've been holding their breath. They look at the screen and watch the stars fill and YES! 3 stars! Piano Maestro will automatically go to a screen where you can take a picture of your student and fill in a short postcard to memorialize the moment.

At the top you can enter an email or if you have already added the student's parent's email it will show automatically. You can type what ever you want in the message section but it has a default message there too.

A Share the Moment with friends at MTNA 2015

My Maestros like to photo bomb each other if they can. Sometimes my student will make goofy faces or super serious faces. Parents love to receive these!

Share the Moment NCKP 2015

What happens next is pretty cool! The page you just created gets sent to the email address on the page. The recipient opens the email to the pictures of the student and an mp3 file of the song that they just successfully played.

*Important Note: Be sure that YOU are quiet during these sessions! Piano Maestro records everything heard in the room during the "play" session. So if you shout "COME ON IN Y'ALL!" in the middle of a child's song. Yup! Those lovely dulcet tones of yours will be included in Mom and Dad's recording. I'm just giving you a friendly warning!

Remember that this is just a picture and an audio recording. It is not a video. These recordings are all saved in the student's file and when the parent clicks on the link embedded in the email they will see a list of ALL the recordings they have been sent. Some parents like to forward these Share the Moment emails to friends and relatives who may not get the chance to attend a recital. Teachers have told me that they forward all the Share the Moments to themselves and then create a Master Link page they send to parents at the end of the year.

I am not a crafty person. I am incapable of creating cool ornaments and binder covers for my students. For Christmas last year I had all the kiddo's learn a few Christmas songs from the Piano Maestro Library and we sent those as AUDIO CHRISTMAS CARDS to their parents the week before Christmas Vacation. Tremendous success and no paper, glue, scissors or glitter was involved. I was rather sad about the glitter.

Section 15
The Teacher Report
Ah this! This is one of my favorite parts of the JoyTunes experience. This is what your email looks

like when you get it. It starts with your Star Student of the Week!

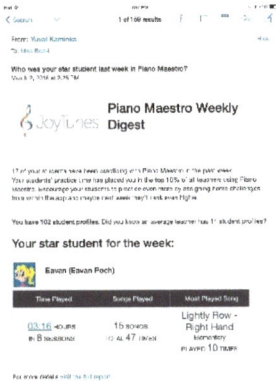

Every Sunday all registered teachers get a Piano Maestro report. The TEACHER REPORT! The teacher report gives you all kinds of information on your students. First, it starts with "Your Maestro of the week was". I feel a contest coming on! Then you tap on the "Show full report" and BooYah! (See image 3 below) All your students, connected and unconnected, show up. All their progress shows! If they play through the song or if they do the learn mode steps, I get to see it ALL! I love this report for ever so many reasons. I love that I can see what interests my students. I get the opportunity to see what they will choose from the library when they are alone. I see how much initiative they have. I can see if they actually did the homework I assigned. I can see how they manage their frustration. I can see what level they actually are.

Some things to remember: Piano Maestro only counts the time they spend playing. It doesn't count the time they spend SEARCHING FOR A SONG! (Insert face palm- I hate watching people try to make a decision. Sends me right around the bend. I much prefer that they do that at home). If they use learn mode you will see it. This is great information for you because it means they are learning to learn. YAY! You can even see if they watched the video tutorials. This is TEACHER NIRVANA!

Image 2

Image 3

It's like actually being the fly on the wall while they practice!

The report is updated every time Piano Maestro is force closed and reopened by either the teacher or the player. If you teach your full day and shut off your iPad with Piano Maestro still running, Apple thinks you are still using the app. You must force close it so the iPad knows you are done. If you are in a Wi-Fi area that will push the day's Piano Maestro progress from all the student's to the JoyTunes servers. Your students also need to force close Piano Maestro from their iPads while connected to Wi-Fi. This is REALLY REALLY important! If you are running a contest and the student doesn't close the app so that practice time can get pushed it won't be counted in the report. THIS IS CRITICAL TO KNOW!

Section 16
Teacher's Kids & Piano Maestro

This is your introduction to hacking. Ok. Not really. It's more like tricking Piano Maestro.

If you have kids of your own and you want them to use Piano Maestro you can add them to your account.   The problem is that you want to assign them home challenges. You can't connect them with your teacher email because it's already being used. So, the hack: you type your email address with +teacher to it.
Example: becki@gmail.com becomes becki+teacher@gmail.com.

When you do this, you won't see any changes. It will look like nothing has happened.   But you'll be able to assign home challenges to your own kids.

Section 17
Apps I LOVE

Among the many outstanding features of JoyTunes are the people who work there. I sent this book out to one of my buddies, Alon to see what he thought and he replied with: "It's GREAT! Please add a chapter on all the cool apps you use too because people might want that information."

How could I say no to a fellow who put Happy from Despicable Me into Piano Maestro because my beloved daughter, Millie, requested it? I can't.

Here is my list of favorite, use them all the time, simply CAN.NOT. Teach without them, apps!

Piano Dust Buster 2
Simply Piano
JoyTunes Metronome
Sprout Beat
Audio Ninja
NinGenius
InFocus Pro

That's the list. This is the why by app name.

Piano Dust Buster 2

This app is by JoyTunes. It is a beginner app and has no educational pedagogy involved. You get 3 pieces to play and your score puts you on a leader board against other persons in your rank and ability. Yes. You are competing with the WORLD. This is why I love it. First of all, I am extremely competitive. Secondly, I have a group of kids who are also all about the COMPETITION! We work at beating each other. We work at beating other countries and sometimes, actual people. Designed for beginners, you have the option of playing just the keys or playing with staff notation.

Another super important thing to note is that while Piano Maestro is only available for iPad, iPad mini and iPad pro, Piano Dust Buster 2 is available for iPods and iPhones too! Thus, putting it within reach of more kids.

Simply Piano

Simply Piano is JoyTune's newest release. It's like a free-style learning system that combines standard pedagogy and contemporary music. It's not a cartoon and harnesses the power of video to help people, mostly adults, learn to play piano. This is designed for iPhones but can be used on iPads as well. It moves fast.

The JoyTunes Metronome
Ok- I got this because I have an Apple watch. I love it. I can set up tempos quickly and the sound of the metronome is nice. Plus it looks really really cool blinking away on my wrist.

SproutBeat
SproutBeat is not an app by JoyTunes but is in the iPad app store. It's a music theory worksheet app. You know how you get all your students a theory book and pray that they will actually do the assignment; then you are routinely disappointed because the dog ate the book, the child hid it in the piano or they just "forgot" it, on purpose, 17 weeks in a row? This is the solution to all of that. Priced at $20 it will be the last theory book you ever buy. Students can do their theory worksheets in your presence on your iPad. It is currently in development to add a student subscription so they can do the assignments at home, send you a screen shot and FINALLY, no more forgetting.

Audio Ninja

My first choice for internalizing rhythm is The Most Addicting Sheep Game. It is no longer available. This is a FANTABULASTIC alternative. Audio Ninja is so so good for little musicians to learn to internalize rhythm. It does not look like a music game and it doesn't do any individual tracking but it is my go to game for getting my students to understand that they have to play and listen and the same time. My kiddos will often beg their parents for the app and play at home. It's really a lot of fun. Once they beat all the levels I move them over to Geometry Dash, which is similar but gives me a headahce.

NinGenius

NinGenius is a very new (as of this writing it was still in its 1.0 version) note-drilling app. I love that I can purchase this 3 different ways. Each student has his or her own profile and I can choose whichever facet I want drilled.   It's a little Ninja kicking away at a board, which gets weaker every time you identify the note correctly. It's a timed game. It also shows a leader board that my students LOVE. We're competitive like that!

InFocus Pro (iPhone app, but works on iPad)

I hate paper. I know it's not politically correct to use the word hate but I really hate paper. It gets everywhere. It stacks up. It makes you feel guilty. It needs constant attention. It is always THERE! I adore this app for making my student records paper free.

I've been on the hunt for the perfect app for me. App purchasing is very personal. It's one of those things that, while one app may work for you, it won't work for someone else. Like, perfume. My old favorite was an app called Penultimate. I loved it because every page was a new lesson and I could add pics and screenshots and I could write in gazillions of colors and doodle and it was wonderful. I was happy. The developers decided to "update" it. Then it was useless. UTTERLY USELESS!

I finally found InFocus Pro. This totally works for me. It's like having a mini file cabinet in your iPad. I know. I know. Evernote, Notability, My Music Staff people are all clamoring… "But you should try those". I did. They didn't work for me. Evernote confuses me. Notability is just not pretty. My Music Staff is too time consuming to set up. I'm telling you… I searched. I tried everything to find the perfect Becki fit. InFocus Pro is it for me.

I made every student a project. Within each project I have files for: weekly assignments, scales, repertoire, recital pieces, exam info. In each file are sub files dated by year, for example: Assignments has files 2014 with each month in another sub sub file. Repertoire: 2014, 2015 and so on. It makes things really easy for me to create subtitute lesson plans. It's great to be able to see everything in one place when I am curriculum planning. I can't be fooled by a student who thinks they can play the same song 2 recitals in a row because I can see their history in their file.

The only con I have for this app is that it is device specific. That means you can't hand off to another device unless you sync your devices with your computer. I have had to commit to using my iPad for all student notes. It's just that one little thing and it wasn't enough to be a deal breaker for me. I can add pictures, doodles, and to do's in this one app. I mail assignment sheets to parents. I dictate my notes so I don't even have to type. I love it.

Since I'm talking about a paperless studio, here's a link to the webinar JoyTunes hosted where I talk

about all the ways you too can be paperless:
https://youtu.be/UrNzyG_uAX4

Section 18
ODDS AND ENDS

This section is basically a random FAQ and insider information.

If you don't know the story of how JoyTunes was founded this is the short version.
Yuval goes to his nephew's house and hears his sister in law say to his nephew "Go Practice piano and show your uncle what you've been learning."

Nephew says, "I'd rather show him my new Wii."

That one statement and JoyTunes is born. Yigal and his brother, Yuval and friend Roey decide to harness the power of gaming and turn it into something that will revolutionize music education. I use it everyday and every time I open Piano Maestro I say a little prayer and ask for blessings upon the JoyTunes family. I puddle like a Seattle storm when I remember the day they said, "free for teachers". I puddle when I see a student who has struggled and struggled light up like Christmas when he gets his 3 stars. I puddle when I see the pride in a parent's face because their baby is a musician. This app is unparalleled in the music industry and we are so lucky to have it.
Thank you gentlemen! Thank you from the very bottom of my heart!

Deleting a Student and Why
There may come a day when you have to delete a student. It's a very easy thing to do. Go to MANAGE

MY STUDENTS tap and under the Red Bar you'll see REMOVE in gray. Tap it and pick the student you need to delete. Carefully. You don't want your finger to slip and take out someone unintentionally. I use a stylus for this because I have stubby, not skinny fingers. Done. See? Easy!

Please note that you are merely deleting them from your studio list. Since they were attached to you they had free access. Once they are deleted from your account, they are no longer eligible for free access until and unless they take lessons with another JoyTunes teacher.

Their progress, though, has not been deleted. They can choose to subscribe and continue the journey on their own if they want.

Use your power for good!

Content Director: Yigal Kaminka is the brains and talent behind the backing tracks. He is the principal Oboist of the Jerusalem Symphony and tours all over the world. He is the reason for the gorgeous tracks for Journey Level songs.

CEO Yuval Kaminka keeps everyone on task and moving. He makes them work in 2-week sprints. This was a concept I had never heard of but MAN! They check off a TON of things from the TO DO LIST under his guidance and direction. He's a really cool guy! I hope I get to meet him one day!

Alon: On the Content Development Team. He is an award winning composer, lecturer and musician. He writes original sound tracks for games and authors. He is also really funny and a foodie.

Mya is the community coordinator. She is the one who schedules webinars and handles teacher requests. She is basically our advocate and our voice. I appreciate so much all the tasks she handles for us. When she sleeps, Linda Christensen, David Love or I forward requests or answer questions.

Nadia is head of Brand Marketing. From England she is now living and working in Israel promoting and getting the word out to the masses about the awesome that is JoyTunes. Not gonna lie. I think she has one of the easiest and hardest jobs there. I mean, Piano Maestro is easy to sell. Finding the people to talk about it? That's hard! She is so wonderful and doesn't ever laugh at my JoyTunes branding, whether it's my Apple watchband or an out of control RED COWBOY HAT. Well, she doesn't laugh where I can see or hear her.

Names you might see tagged for Technical questions:
Lior, Yoni, Oded, Matan, Lital- These are the DEV DUDES! Stop by the JoyTunes Teacher page and give them a shout out! They are the masterminds of the actual coding of the app. The only insider info I can give you about them is that I irritate Lior the most, what with my constant questions, frizzing my hair ideas and opinions and what not!

JTT: JoyTunes Teacher Facebook page
The coolest, bestest group on Facebook. This is the place where you go when you want to make a song suggestion, report a problem or glitch, or show off a student video. It's a happy place!

Important iPad Basic Function (iiBF): If you double tap the iPad home button (the circle button located at the bottom of the ipad screen on the actual iPad which I also call the iPad belly button) all your open apps will show as thumbnail pics. You can choose to switch between these apps by tapping the picture of the app you want.

My student's account is locked.
I hear this often. I am never really sure what it means.

Let's start with this scenario. Student accounts are supposed to show locks in the Journey section. They have to unlock each level. Like Tomb Raider or Grand Tourismo all the upcoming levels are LOCKED because you haven't earned your way into them yet. Once you begin to acquire stars, they accumulate and when you have enough the next level will unlock.

The other way Piano Maestro looks locked is if the parent or student didn't connect properly. This shows when you go to the library and you can't see any of the methods or Pop & Rock tunes. It means that Apple is waiting for this account to become a subscriber. If this is your student then they are not connected. See the Chapter titled: GETTING CONNECTED

Now, you, the teacher, open your iPad, open Piano Maestro and you see a blinking circle in Manage my Students. You tap and approve the request. Now, one last step. Both sides need to force close the app and reopen Piano Maestro. (See chapter Getting Started) Again, remember that the only way JoyTunes servers know what is going on is if you close Piano Maestro completely and reopen it. Not delete and reinstall. This is just a normal "close because I'm done using it". This stores all the current progress in the cloud and when someone opens the account, Piano Maestro gets that information pushed to whoever opens it next.

I'm not a beginner. How do I skip ahead?
Good one! In the upper right corner in every Journey Chapter up to chapter 27 is a fast forward button. That's 2 right pointing arrows and a Chapter number. This is "fast forward to Chapter 5". This is a legit test of skill. No messing around either. You must get 3 stars (90% better in notation and rhythm) or you don't pass and you stay put. A whole new meaning to No Pass NO play!

My blue tooth speaker doesn't work well with Piano Maestro. How come?
I don't know. I just know it doesn't. It's something about the iPad can't process Bluetooth and listen and process incoming sound all at the same time.

Speakers work just fine when plugged into the iPad. I like using speakers a lot because the sound is bigger and richer and it makes for a more wonderful experience. The iPad Pro has such great speakers this is completely unnecessary!

Piano Maestro opens and then immediately closes. Whizzah Whuzzah?
This is an Apple thing. When Apple does their updates so do the developers. They have to make the new Apple changes work in their apps, That means that if you don't do the Apple update then you run the risk of locking up Piano Maestro because it is searching for an operating command that isn't there.

This is the official link to the FAQ's on the JoyTunes page:

https://teachers.joytunes.com/faq

Take a minute and browse the JoyTunes website. There are teacher guides, parent guides, webinars, youtube videos, tutorials, and printables.

I told you! Odds and Ends! I have ADD. I make no apologies. You're lucky this book is as organized as it is.

SECTION 19
PIANO MAESTRO MEETS THE GROUP CLASS!
Webinar Link: https://youtu.be/PXs7OpFkCuQ

I just did (January 2016) a webinar on how to use Piano Maestro in a group class. These are my notes. I'm adding them in here so you can have a reference but really you should hunt down the webinar (google Piano Maestro Meets the Group Class) and watch and listen. The webinar has slides that are really helpful and less "list-y".

I'm going into this with a couple of assumptions. Yes. I said assumptions. 1. That you already know how Piano Maestro works on both acoustic and digi pianos and uses no cables. I'm also assuming that you have a teacher account. You should know that JoyTunes give Piano Maestro to teachers and their students for FREE! Take that in a moment. Doesn't matter how many students you have. 3 or 500… no limits on the number of students you can have on your account. I just don't want to have to look at your teacher report because it is going to be MASSIVE!

Setting up Large Classes for Piano Maestro
I've talked to a lot of teachers and do you know? Everyone has a different scenario. I'm going to do a couple so you can see some options but do know that since Piano Maestro isn't optimized for large group classes you really can do whatever you want. I'm just here to get you started.

3 scenarios:
    a. 1:1 iPad school, each child is issued an iPad and has an email assigned to them by the school
    b. Cart iPads: one set of ipads shared by all teachers, students do not have school issued ipad

c. 1 teacher ipad to teach the group.

I promise I know that there are a gazillion different combinations but we'll stick with these for now.

Usually, for the private teacher it works like this: new student arrives, teacher adds new student to her account, teacher sends an emailed invitation to parents to download Piano Maestro on their iPad at home (I'm not going into the 3 thousand ways the parents do it wrong), the email is tagged in the JT servers so when the account is created, the student is automatically connected. No extra steps.

I said that really fast but there are always ways to make a mistake. This is the ideal, BEST case scenario.

But this is not for us. Do you really want to type in 500 student emails? You can. You could. I have ADD so I'd totally lose track of my thought and mess up after like 2. What are the odds you mis-type? So we are going to go the back route.

Scenario A: 1:1 iPad school.
Usually in this scenario the teacher has to request from the IT department that Piano Maestro be downloaded to everyone's iPad. That's the easy part. Now we have to figure out how to get everyone an account. This is just "create an account" but walking the whole class through the log in process. In this situation I recommend doing it backwards to

save yourself the hassle of having to send invitations to every student.

Step 1: Every student goes to the Log In Screen and taps GET STARTED. You must be in a wifi area.

Step 2: They all tap: "I'm over 13 and using the app myself"

Step 3: They all type in the information that is unique to them. First name, Last name, email and then a universal password.

TIME OUT!
HOW TO NAME YOUR STUDENTS

 You have to be able to find your students quickly and Piano Maestro does alphabetize the students. This can work to your advantage if you think through how you want your classes to show.   The First name field can be THE DAY and TIME of the Class and the Last Name field can be The Childs First name and last initial.   In your MY ACCOUNT you will only see the first name field.

For example:

First name   CamilleL,T930

Last name: School district, your last name, whatever.

Another possible formula would be:

Day/Time, StudentFirst and Last name (W1130 YoniT)

This will only work in the scenario I described where the student's create their accounts and connect to you manually.   If you try to go back and do this later You will not be able to separate the First and Last name. Notice that in the slides only the First Name shows. For this reason you'll need to play around with how you want to see your student list when you look at the whole thing. It's also really fantastic if you work a class schedule where you see the same kids on the same day throughout the year. But if that's not the case for you can always go back into MANAGE MY STUDENTS and change the lesson days.

A NOTE ABOUT PASSWORDS FOR CLASSES (and private students too)

I have ALL my students use the same password. This way if I ever need to go into their account to fix something I'm not asking for a password and I can never be accused of knowing their icloud or bank passwords- because you know they do that. For the sake of this webinar, let's say the Password is WEBinar but you can choose whatever you like. Once they hit CREATE ACCOUNT. They are in. The next step is critical to ensure there are no charges for any student. DON'T MISS THIS NEXT STEP!

(Again, normally, I don't do things this way but unless you want to spend your whole weekend entering a bunch of student emails, this will be the easiest way to do this with a minimal amount of errors. I hope.)

Step 4: Every student taps the RED MY ACCOUNT button in the upper right corner.
They will see a screen that says Teachers & Parents ZONE >Profiles. On the left side they will see their name, avatar, rank and the phrase "NOT CONNECTED".

Step 5: Tap the students name so the profile details show on the right side.

Step 6: They can change their pic by tapping the picture, and changing the age if they want.

Step 7: Everyone taps the GREEN CONNECT TO TEACHER button at the bottom.

Step 8: A search menu appears. Students then type YOUR email in that box.

Step 9: Hopefully there is only one of you. They need to tap your name.

Step 10: Your info should appear in a box on the right with a GREEN CONNECT button at the bottom.

Step 11: TAP THE GREEN BUTTON!

Step 12: The screen goes away and the students see the box change to CONNECTION STATUS, in yellow letters Waiting for YOUR NAME. Your teacher needs to approve the invitation.

That's it for the students.

But not for you.

You are going to have to approve all of the students who are requesting connection.

Instructions for you

Step 1: Log in or open Piano Maestro.

Step 2: Go to the RED MANAGE MY STUDENTS which should have a blinking red dot and a giant number of requests. Tap the Red Button.

Step 3: You'll see a Blue Bar that says "Manage Students" and a Red Bar that says YOUR STUDENTS. Below that in a pale yellow you will see

all the students you need to approve. DON'T TAP
YET.
Step 4: If you tap the grey arrow next to the students
name you'll get their name, age, avatar and LESSON
DAY BOX! Tap lesson day and put in the class day
for that student.
Step 5: NOW Push the GREEN APPROVE button.
Step 6: Check the profile box and be sure
CONNECTION STATUS reads (in green letters)
Connected to "Student's Name".

Remember that Piano Maestro will only show the
students you have on any given day the students you
have designated for that day. You CAN open any
student at any time from your iPad but they won't be
using your iPad. Just so you understand how it
works. When they log in to their iPads they will only
see their profile and be able to work on only their
account. You may need to teach them to log in and
out of Piano Maestro.

The great thing about having a 1:1 ipad school is that
each student has their own account and can't mess
up their friend's (or not) account.

Scenario 2:
CART iPads

With a cart of iPads you still need to get IT to
download Piano Maestro to all the iPads. You'll need
to add all your students one at a time but with no
email. This is TOTALLY OK! You won't be able to
assign home challenges but that's ok because they

don't take these ipads home. This will just be for school use.

Step 1: Open Piano Maestro and go to the RED Manage my Students Button and tap it.
Step 2: Tap the blue "+ADD NEW"
Step 3: Type in the student's name in the Nick Name box using whatever formula for your class you like, choose the lesson day and age, change the avatar if you want or make that a class project later.
Step 4: Tap the Green ADD TO ACCOUNT button.
Step 5: Get every iPad and log in to your account so all the students show on your account. The students will need to search the list for their name in every class. No one should be logging out. EVER.

Herein lies the danger of cross contamination. You'll have to instill the fear of YOU so that they don't mess around with someone else's account.

Scenario 3:
You have a school issued iPad and no one but you uses it. You project your apps on a screen, smart board or wall.
For this I recommend naming each class as DAY/Time. Since it's likely that the class will travel as a whole, united group you don't have to worry about individual work. You'll be progressing through the curriculum with each class according to their strengths and abilities. Everyone stays together because they have to.
Step 1: Open Piano Maestro and go to the RED Manage my Students Button and tap it.

Step 2: Tap the blue "+ADD NEW"

Step 3: Type in the class name in the Nick Name box using whatever formula for your class you like, choose the lesson day and leave off the age change the avatar if you want or make that a class project later.   (TUES 10:30 3rd Period/2nd grade), no email.

Step 4: Tap the Green ADD TO ACCOUNT button.

Step 5: Get every iPad and log in to your account

When they have to find their name in the student list, they can type it in the search (magnifying glass at the top of " Start a Lesson with Any Student" and it will show.

SECTION 2
Piano Maestro and Hardware

You've got a couple options here too. Do you have a: 1. piano lab where each student has their own piano/keyboard and each student has an iPad for that piano/keyboard or 2. They all have a piano/keyboard but only you have the iPad.

Again, I know there are lots of combinations here too.

If you have 1 iPad per keyboard and you want them to work on their own account through the Piano Maestro Journey Curriculum or through any of the included curriculums BY THEMSELVES with you floating to help as needed. You'll need to connect each keyboard to the iPad.

For each Piano Station you'll need: a piano or keyboard with Midi connections, an iOS midi cable and a set of headphones.

iConnectMIDI1 for Lightning connector
by iConnectivity
Link: http://amzn.com/B00MRFG3WU
  iConnectMIDI1 for 30 pin connector
by iConnectivity
Link: http://amzn.com/B00D77A8VO

Which cable you purchase depends on the generation of IPad you have.

Headphones: whatever your school district will approve. I prefer over the ear, faux leather (so I can wipe them down).

SETTING UP
Plug the side of the midi cable that matches your iPad into your ipad. The other side has 2 plugger thingies. One is labeled In and one is labled out. On your keyboard you'll need to plug the cable in to the keyboard out and the cable out to the keyboard in. Now check to make sure it works. Again, opposites attract. Most of the time when it doesn't you just need to switch the cables. Next you'll want to plug in the headphones. You'll control all volume from the iPad now so turn the volume down on the piano.

If you have a bunch of keyboards in one room but only 1 ipad you'll need to project your iPad so the kids can see what is being demo'd.   Piano Maestro can hear your piano so you won't need to connect the piano to the monitor. You'll just need to connect the iPad to the monitor. They can play and follow on their keyboards. It is going to be noisy.

USING A PROJECTOR
 Projectors come in all shapes and styles. You'll need to check the owner's manual to see how to connect your projector to your iPad. You should check with your IT guy to make sure you don't get unnecessary cables and adapters.

I have a: ViewSonic PJD5132 SVGA DLP Projector, 3000 Lumens, PC 3D-Ready, 120Hz

This has a couple ways to connect. I can use a VGA connector or an HDMI cable. I prefer the HDMI because it gives me sound through the projector. Then I attach an external speaker to the projector so I get BIG SOUND. Using the VGA connector will only give me the iPad image and I need to add a speaker to the iPad to we can hear it.

Here's a link for the Apple HDMI –Lightning adapter. Then you'll need the appropriate length HDMI cable. One end of this cable goes into the adapter and the other goes to the projector.
http://www.amazon.com/Apple-MD825ZM-Lightning-VGA-Adapter/dp/B00FG2CN70

You'll also need an HDMI cable, like this one.

AmazonBasics High-Speed HDMI Cable - 3 Feet (0.9 Meter)
Supports Ethernet, 3D, 4K and Audio Return

This one is 3 feet but I actually pack a 20 ft and a 12
ft. I move when I teach.

USING A TV or COMPUTER MONITOR to display your iPad

Plug the lightning end into the ipad and connect the
Monitor VGA cable to the other side of the adapter.
Then the other end of the VGA cable into the monitor.

Here's the link for the VGA adapter.

Apple Mini DisplayPort to VGA Adapter MB572Z/B

And the cable you'll need something like this:

Fullink Premium HD15 Male to Male SVGA VGA
Long Video Monitor Cable for TV Computer Projector
3 feet

And you'll need an AUX CABLE for your speaker.
You determine the length.

Super HD 3.5mm Aux Stereo Audio Cable Tangle-Free Slim
Cable Angled Male Type Compatible for Car,Stereo Audio...
You will need to add an external speaker (not
Bluetooth) connected to your iPad so you get sound.

SECTION 3
PIANO MAESTRO and CLASS ACTIVITIES
Some ideas to get you started:

If you have 1:1 ipads, you can demo from yours and have them watch and then play themselves with their headphones.

If you have only one ipad you can demo and then hit restart so the class can play with you. Yes, your iPads mic will hear what everyone is playing. No, it will not be that accurate because the odds are pretty good that the class is going to stutter their way into a good score. This is where your gifted ear comes into play and you decide whether to accept the score or do it again. I always do it at least 3 times to make sure everyone is mostly capable.

If you have a cart, you can demo and then have them play on their own, with headphones or with headphones and keyboards.

If you can't afford to get the midi cables and stuff you can get away with using the Journey and playing with the iPad keyboard on the screen with headphones. It's not easy on the mini because the screen is small but it's ok for most of the beginning levels. Most of those only use 3 or 4 notes. No it's not ideal. Probably yes, they will 2 finger typist when they play because the keys are tiny but it's a start. Take the long view that for now, you are building a program and you can show admin how beneficial this kind of work is for kids. I'm not saying that poor technique is the way to go. I am saying that sometimes we need to set aside the "perfect" for the "lets get them excited".

Here's a class schedule for a 50 minute class:
5-8 minutes: Come in, yell HEY Y'ALL! Sit and get settled, log in…. be happy teacher
2 minute: Teacher Review of class rules (This is SOP for me in every class anyway! I have 4 rules everyone has to learn and repeat).
15 minutes: YOU TEACH THE CONCEPT using off the bench activities.
10 minutes: STUDENT PRACTICE/GROUP PLAY
8-12 minutes: Play Concept taught in Piano Maestro
3-5 minutes: log out, clean up, set up for next class

Here's another class Schedule:
5 minutes: Log in to student account and SIT!
15 minutes: Teach a JOURNEY CHAPTER, Highlight and demo the songs. Be sure to discuss hands playing together and separately, review counting.
15-20 minutes: SOLO PLAY
5 minutes: CLASS Q's and Ask students about their progress
5 minutes: log out, clean up, set up for next class

Teaching a Journey Chapter:
Journey Chapter 1: RH Middle C
Concepts taught in this chapter: Introduction music (when to start), Symbols & Signs they need to know: Treble cleff, ¾ and 4/4 time, staff, double bar lines, half notes, half rests, quarter notes, finger numbers. right hand plays treble clef, keyboard topography (so they can find Middle C to trigger the start to play. You

need to decide which finger you want them to use because it says 1).

TEACH RHYTHMS OFF THE BENCH
On a white board or poster board write out the main rhythms of the Journey Chapter songs. Using a metronome, write these out and jump them. They stand behind their seats and jump the rhythms. (First, full body jumps, then clap, then finger taps)
Flash cards of: Quarters, half notes, half rests... DRILL!
Listening exercises: Vivaldi's Spring, Blue Danube. Clap and sing. Teach them to dance the waltz.

Example of Lesson Plans
Teaching Journey Chapter 9
(this is a random selection)

Concepts: quarter notes, half rests, whole rests, dotted halfs, dotted half rests, quarter rests, half notes, quarter rests, Treble notes: CDE, Bass Notes GAB, Sharp symbol (even though they don't use it) Hands alternate right to left, never together.

Minor Dreams:
FINGER NUMBER DRILL: RH1, RH 3, LH1, LG 2 Do in teams of 2 so they can check each other.
PATTERN PLAY! Start on Treble C- Walk to E, start on Treble E- walk down C, Start on Bass A-walk to C

Fur Elise: Play "CLAP ON X!" They have to clap on 1 of each measure. Then 3 of each measure. Then 1 and 3.

Twinkle: You can divide the class into teams and have them play the music version of 7-UP. Label the teams with Post it's with the letter name on it. When I introduce this game stage 1 I keep the groups together. But to change it up and make it harder (and find the cheaters) we move to stage 2 where I create random teams spread out through the class.

Apologize: Make sure you listen to the radio version and then teach the song. It only uses 4 notes: Treble CD, Bass: GA Have them look for patterns in the music. Start the song and have them look for patterns while you scroll through the song. Also play NAME THAT NOTE while you scroll and point at random notes.

Print this out or project the sheet music so you can all play as a group slowly while you point. You can also play Pin The Post It on the image. Points for student teams that can identify the notes or play them!

As you can see and hear, there's lots of room for your own style. Be you, just MORE! Plan and Play- that's the theme for group classes!

USING THE JOURNEY

The Journey Section of Piano Maestro is really great for getting a class started. Here's the link for you to see the Journey Curriculum:

https://teachers.joytunes.com/assets/guidelines/PM_ ChapterByChapter_Curriculumm.pdf

The first chapters are all Middle C learning based. It's fairly easy to go ahead and teach quarters, half and whole notes and then demo using Chapter 1 Rocking. Once you get started the kids will get really excited and BEG you to let them try.

If everyone has an iPad you can let them work on their own. I have my classes complete chapter 1 and then they have to wait for everyone else. Or they can keep practicing those songs until everyone catches up. I know. You can only move as fast as the slowest kid. Everyone knows this. Including the kids. If you have some more mature kids who want to help the others I let them as long as they 1. Use kind words and 2. DON'T DO THE WORK FOR THE OTHER KID!

You can also commit to using a Method series. Lucky for you the Music Magicians at JoyTunes have given you several to choose from.

If you can (and I'd totally recommend it but I realize money doesn't grow on trees) use Jennifer Eklund's Piano Pronto or Use Alfred's Premier Piano Course. Both of these series are great for group classes. The books are super helpful because the lesson is planned for you and all you have to do is expand it for a class. Teaching quarter notes? Explain it your way, practice tapping body rhythms, then play those pieces in the book and then do them in Piano Maestro.

I know you all have your own methods for teaching piano topography and I would definitely do that first (so they can find Middle C). In fact one of our favorite games is to play all the c's on the keyboard (because that's the highlighted start key) and have them watch the screen until it BINGS. Then they have to put a pompom on the key so they can remember where it is. I might let them throw those at each other when class is over.

Once you've got them started you'll find your own teaching rhythm pretty easily. Keep going and just remember every class will have it's own pace.

OTHER QUICK TIPS!
One of my other favorite things to do is to have one child do the song treble clef only and another child do bass clef. Sort of a duet but not really… It's fun for them to learn team work.

Other times I will have them work on a song then divide the group into teams. I line them up in 2 rows. The first 2 in each individual line come to the piano and they play a short song or exercise. I write down the score for each individual. Highest SCORE, not percentage, gets the point. GO TEAM!

Shutting Down

This is the end my friends. We are about done with this conversation.

Shutting down Piano Maestro

One final reminder that when you are done with Piano Maestro for the day you should force close it. See GETTING STARTED if you forgot how. Actually, I force close every 2 hours to maintain top, peak performance.

Sometimes iPad files get contaminated with data getting put in weird places. Do you remember having to defrag your computer? Basically the same thing happens to iPad. As you open apps, iPad uses whatever space is available wherever it can find it. Sometimes things get slotted wrong and when that happens you get weird glitches. Things like, your graphics are missing big chunks or Piano Maestro backing tracks hiccup or the scrolling sheet music stutters. These are all things that happen to the iPad. Nothing is wrong with Piano Maestro. To fix most of these issues: force close all open apps. Turn the iPad off for 3-5 minutes. Turn it back on and reopen Piano Maestro.

If something REALLY ODD is going on you may be asked to DELETE and REINSTALL. This is no big deal. Seriously. Just tap and hold the Piano Maestro icon until it starts to wiggle. Then tap the x to make it go away (delete it). Open the App store app, search Piano Maestro and download it again.

Don't worry. Your data is safe. Student info is stored in the cloud. Your account is safely held in the JoyTunes cloud. Log In and your account is just as it was. If you had previously downloaded content for use off line, you'll have to do that again.

I know. Bummer.

Shutting down Part 2

Well, campers, this is it. The end. Time for me to leave the stage. Thank you for sticking it out with me. I hope this book helps make your personal Piano Maestro and Apple journeys a little easier. I'm sorry all you grammerists (yes, I know you are out there) for my excessive use of parentheses, exclamation points and other grammatical irritants.

You can always find me online in Facebook: Becki JoyTunes Maestro Laurent. And if you spend anytime on the JoyTunes Teacher page you'll see me lurking. I lurk all the time.

If you need any help at all feel free to contact me at: becki.laurent@joytunes.com. JoyTunes was so gracious to give me an email address. Cool, right?

As I leave I need to thank a couple "insiders". I met Marta Mozes when I wrote a letter to JoyTunes thanking them for a "game changer." It was Piano Dustbuster. She is a wonderful person, a good friend and I wouldn't be writing this book if not for her.

I also need to thank Yigal and Yuval Kaminka and Roey Izkovsky for bringing us Piano Maestro in the first place. If not for their vision, talent and time... well, we wouldn't be using this fantastic app and changing musical lives.

I also need to thank Donna Fisher. I met her a few years ago while working at a private school. Life happens and before you know it, BAM! She and I work together again. She is my right arm and a woman of many talents. Among them, she is a legit writer and editor. She is so much a detail person and I am grateful (and you should be too) that she edited this book and made me correct spacing, bolding and formatting errors. I love her so much and I'm lucky every day to work with her.

And thank YOU for reading my book. I wish you and your students the best, most wonderful lessons using every tool in your teaching toolbox.

With my love and gratitude,

Ms. Becki

www.ingramcontent.com/pod-product-compliance
Lightning Source LLC
Chambersburg PA
CBHW051238090426
42742CB00001B/7